D1524786

Impressionism

Susie Brooks

COMPASS POINT BOOKS
a capstone imprint

Compass Point Books are published by Capstone,
1710 Roe Crest Drive, North Mankato, Minnesota 56003
www.mycapstone.com

Library of Congress Cataloging-in-Publication Data
Names: Brooks, Susie, author.
Title: Impressionism / by Susie Brooks.
Description: North Mankato, Minnesota : Compass Point Books, a Capstone
   imprint, [2020] | Series: Inside art movements | Audience: 9-14. |
   Audience: 4 to 6.
Identifiers: LCCN 2018060763 | ISBN 9780756562373 (hardcover)
Subjects: LCSH: Impressionism (Art)—Juvenile literature. | Art, Modern—19th
   century—Juvenile literature.
Classification: LCC N6465.I4 B76 2020 | DDC 709.03/44—dc23
LC record available at https://lccn.loc.gov/2018060763

Editorial credits
Series editor: Julia Bird
Designer: Mo Choy Design Ltd.
Image research: Diana Morris

Image credits:
front cover. Claude Monet, Poppies at Argenteuil detail, 1873, oil on canvas, 50 x 65 cm, Musée d'Orsay, Paris. Superstock. 1. Claude Monet, Poppies at Argenteuil detail, 1873, oil on canvas ,50 x 65 cm, Musée d'Orsay, Paris. Superstock. 3. Edgar Degas, Mary Cassatt at the Louvre 1885, Pastel over etching, mixed media on paper, 31.3 x 13.7 cm, Art Institute Chicago. Bridgeman Images.4. Auguste Renoir, The Skiff (Boating on the Seine), 1875, oil on canvas, 71 x 92 cm, National Gallery, London. A Burkatovski/ Fine Art Images/Superstock. 5. Edgar Degas, The Millinery Shop, 1879-86, oil on canvas, 100 x 110.7 cm, The Art Institute of Chicago, Mr & Mrs Lewis Larned Coburn Memorial Collection. Bridgeman Images. 6. Édouard Manet by Nadar, c.1875, photograph. Pictorial Press/Alamy. 7t. Frédéric Bazille, Studio in the Rue La Condamine, 1870, oil on canvas, 98 x 128.5 cm, Musée d'Orsay, Paris. ArtArchive/Superstock. 7b. Edouard Manet, Music at the Tuilleries, 1862, oil on canvas, 76.2 x 118.1 cm, National Gallery, London. Bridgeman/Superstock. 8t. Camille Corot painting en plein air c. 1860, photograph. Everett Historical/Shutterstock. 8b. Camille Corot, Oak Trees at Bas-Bréau, Fontainbleau, 1832-3, oil on paper laid down on wood, 39.7 x 49.5 cm, Metropolitan Museum, New York. PD/Wikimedia Commons. 9. Camille Pissarro, Hermitage at Pontoise, c. 1867, oil on canvas, 151.4 x200.6 cm, Solomon R. Guggenheim Museum, New York. Artepics/age fotostock/ Superstock. 10. Claude Monet, The Beach at Trouville, 1870, oil on canvas, 38 x 46.5 cm, National Gallery, London. Bridgeman Images. 11. Eugène Boudin, The Beach at Trouville, 1865, oil on cardboard, 26.5 x 40.5 cm, Musée d'Orsay, Paris. 4 x 5 Collection/Superstock. 12t. Paul Delaroche, Hémicycle, section 2, 1841-2 oil and wax fresco, Ecole des Beaux-Arts, Paris. PD/ Wikimedia Commons. 12b. Jean-François Millet, Man with a Hoe, c.1861, oil on canvas, 81.9 x 100.3 cm, J. Paul Getty Museum, Los Angeles. Superstock. 13. Edouard Manet, Déjeuner sur l'herbe, 1863, oil on canvas, 208 x 264 cm, Musée d'Orsay, Paris. 4 x 5 Collection/Superstock. 14. Claude Monet, Impression, Sunrise, 1872, oil on canvas, 48 x 63 cm, Musée Marmottan, Paris. akg/Superstock. 15. Berthe Morisot, The Cradle, 1872, oil on canvas, 56 x 46 cm, Musée d'Orsay, Paris. Superstock. 16c. Michel Chevreul chromatic circle, 1839, Didot, Paris. 16b. Alfred Sisley, The Effect of Snow at Argenteuil, 1874, oil on canvas, 54 x 65 cm, Musée d'Orsay, Paris. Bridgeman Images. 17. Camille Pissarro, The Artist's Palette with Landscape, c. 18778-80, oil on wood, 24.1 x 34.6 cm, Clark Art Institute, Williamstown, MA. Bridgeman Images. 18cl.Gustave Caillbotte, Rainy Day, 1877, oil on canvas, 212.2 x 276.2 cm, Art Institute, Chicago. A Burkatovski/Fine Art Images/Superstock. 18cr. Claude Monet, Boulevarde des Capucines, 1873, oil on canvas, 80.3 x 60.3 cm, Nelson Atkins Museum of Art, Kansas City. Classic Paintings/Alamy. 19. Auguste Renoir, Bal au Moulin de la Galette, 1876, oil on canvas, 131 x 175 cm, Musée d'Orsay, Paris. Tolo Balaguer/age fotostock/Superstock. 20t. Edouard Manet, Monet on his studio boat, 1874, oil on canvas, 80 x 98 cm, Neue Pinakothek, Munich. De Agostini/Superstock. 20b. Alfred Sisley, Boat in the Flood at Port Marly, 1876, oil on canvas, 61 x 50.5 cm, Musée d'Orsay, Paris. De Agostini/Superstock. 21. James McNeill Whistler, Nocturne: Blue and Gold-Old Battersea Bridge, c. 1872-5, oil on canvas, 68 x 51 cm, Tate, London. De Agostini/Superstock. 22. Camille Pissarro, The Côtes des Boeufs at L'Hermitage, 1877, oil on canvas, 114.9 x 87.6 cm, National Gallery, London. Artepics/age fotostock/Superstock. 23. Paul Cézanne, La Côte Saint-Denis à Pontoise, c. 1877, oil on canvas, 65.4 x 54.2 cm, Private Collection, on loan Museum of Fine Arts, St Petersburg, Florida.Christies. 24. Camille Pissarro, Lordship Lane Station, Dulwich, 1871, oil on canvas 44.5 x 72.5 cm, Courtauld Gallery, London. De Agostini/Superstock. 25t. Claude Monet, Gare Saint-Lazare, 1877, oil on canvas, 75 x 105 cm, Musée d'Orsay, Paris. A Burkatovski/Fine Art Images/Superstock. 25b. J M W Turner, Rain, Speed and Steam, The Great Western Railway, 1844, oil on canvas, 91 x 121.8cm, National Gallery, London. Peter Barritt/Superstock. 26. Edweard Muybridge, Horse Galloping, 1878, photograph. PD/Wikimedia Commons. 27t. Edgar Degas, At the Races, 1877-80, oil on canvas, 66 x 81 cm, Musée d'Orsay, Paris. Interfoto/Superstock. 27b. Auguste Renoir, At the Theatre (La Première Sortie), 1876-7 oil on canvas 65 x 49.5 cm, National Gallery, London. Peter Barritt/Superstock. 28. Edgar Degas in 1917, photograph. Chronicle/Alamy. 29. Edgar Degas, The Star (L'Etoile), 1878, pastel on monotype, 58.4 x 42 cm, Musée d'Orsay, Paris. 4 x 5 Collection/Superstock. 30. Mary Cassatt, Little Girl in Blue Armchair, 1878, oil on canvas, 88 x 128.5, National Gallery of Art, Washington D.C. Quint Lox Ltd/Superstock. 31. Berthe Morisot, Summer's Day, c.1879, oil on canvas, 45.7 x 75.2 cm, National Gallery, London. A Burkatovski/Fine Art Images/Superstock. 32. Auguste Renoir c .1875, photograph. PD/Wikimedia Commons. 33. Auguste Renoir, Luncheon of the Boating Party, 1881, oil on canvas, 130 x 175 cm, Phillips Collection, Washington D.C.3HL/Superstock. 34. Tanaka Masunobu, Young man playing a flute c 1740-50, woodblock on paper, pillar print. PD/ Wikimedia Commons. 35bl. Mary Cassatt, Woman Bathing, c. 1891 drypoint and aquatint, 43.2 x 29.8 cm, Metropolitan Museum, New York. PD. 35tr. Edgar Degas, Mary Cassatt at the Louvre 1885, pastel over etching, mixed media on paper, 31.3 x 13.7 cm, Art Institute Chicago. Bridgeman Images. 36. Paul Durand-Ruel, photograph. PD/Wikimedia Commons. 37. Camille Pissarro, Fan Mount: The Cabbage Gatherers, c. 1878-9, gouache on silk, 16.5 x 52.1 cm, Metropolitan Museum, New York. PD. 38. Georges Seurat, A Sunday Afternoon on the Island of La Grande Jatte, 1884-6, oil on canvas, 207.65 x 307.1 cm, Art Institute of Chicago PD/Wikimedia Commons. 39. Vincent Van Gogh, The Starry Night, 1889, oil on canvas, 73.7 x 92.1 cm, Museum of Modern Art, New York. PD/Wikimedia Commons. 40. Claude Monet, Nympheas, 1914-17, oil on canvas, 150 x 200 cm, Musée Marmottan, Paris. Peter Barritt/Superstock. 41. Woman looking at Monet's Waterlilies in l'Orangerie, Paris, photograph. Martin Child/Robert Harding PL. 42bl. Theodore Robinson, The Wedding March, 1892, oil on canvas, 56 x 67.3 cm, Terra Foundation for American Art. PD/Wikimedia Commons. 42cr. Phillip Wilson Steer, Boulogne Sands, 1888-91, oil on canvas, 61 x 76.5 cm, Tate, London. PD/Wikimedia Commons. 43. Charles Condor, Centennial Choir at Sorrento, 1889, oil on panel, 10.5 x 23.5 cm, Private Collection. PD/Wikimedia Commons. 44. Paul Cézanne, Mont Saint-Victoire, 1902-4, oil on canvas, 69.8 x 89.5 cm, Philadelphia Museum of Art. PD/Wikimedia Commons. 45t. Jackson Pollock, Reflection of the Big Dipper,1947, paint on canvas, 111 x 91.5 cm, Stedelijk Museum, Amsterdam. © The Pollock-Krasner Foundation/ARS, NY and DACS, London 2018. Universal History Archive/ Getty Images. 45bl. Roy Lichtenstein, Rouen Cathedral from Set 5, 1969, oil and magma on canvas, 161.61 x 120.12 cm, SFMOMA. © The Estate of Roy Lichtenstein/DACS, London 2018, 45br. Claude Monet, Rouen Cathedral, West Façade, Sunlight, 1894, oil on canvas, 100 x 65.8 cm, National Gallery of Art, Washington, D.C. Everett Art/Shutterstock.

First published in Great Britain in 2018 by Wayland
Copyright © Hodder & Stoughton, 2018

All internet sites appearing in back matter were available and accurate when this book was sent to press.

Printed and bound in China.
1593

Table of Contents

Making an Impression

With their bold flicks of paint and adventurous colors, the impressionists certainly made an impression! When they first started painting, their work was difficult for many people to accept—but it has since become an international success story.

What Is Impressionism?

Impressionism was an art movement that grew up in the late 1860s among a group of artists in Paris, France. The world around them was changing fast, and they wanted their art to match this. So they painted in a way that no one had seen before, using unblended brushstrokes and daring compositions. They worked outdoors, took inspiration from modern life, and shocked people with their sketchy style.

A New Realism

Before the impressionists most artists tried to paint realistically. From the 1850s a group called the realists went a step further, painting ordinary people in everyday landscapes—nothing heroic like the classical or romantic scenes of the past. This honesty impressed the impressionists, but they wanted something new. They wanted to put the fleeting effects of light and nature on canvas.

The Skiff (Boating on the Seine), Pierre-Auguste Renoir, 1875

Capturing Moments

Look at the bright, bold flecks of color and the hazy figures in *The Skiff (Boating on the Seine)* (above). Auguste Renoir, who painted this, was one of the leading impressionists. When he propped up his easel by the river, he aimed to sum up a passing moment. He tried to capture the flickering feel of sunlight with his swift, broken strokes of paint.

A Diverse Group

Other impressionist painters included Claude Monet, Camille Pissarro, Alfred Sisley, Edgar Degas, and Berthe Morisot. While they all shared similar ideas and influences, they were very much individuals. Degas, for example, barely ever painted outdoors but focused on the human aspect of modern life. He drew dancers, racehorses, housewives, shops, and circus acts—working mainly from his indoor studio.

The Millinery Shop, Edgar Degas, 1879–1886

Look Closer

In traditional painting, figures or narrative features usually took center stage. Look at the viewpoint and use of space the painting above. Can you see why scenes like this seemed unusual for the time?

Friends in Paris

Most of the future impressionists met in teaching studios in Paris in the late 1850s and early 1860s. They became friends, living and socializing in the lively Batignolles district along with other avant-garde artists and writers.

Manet's Café Crowd

One person the group looked up to was Édouard Manet. This pioneering painter held noisy evening debates at the local Café Guerbois, where writers such as Émile Zola were among the crowd. Zola wrote articles championing the impressionists. But in 1886 he wrote his novel *The Masterpiece*, which told the story of a failed artist. This lost him a friend in Paul Cézanne, on whom the novel seemed to be based on.

Student Life

By day the artists worked in their various studios. Some studied with the painter Charles Gleyre, who taught them classical skills but also gave them the freedom to be original. Others sketched from life models at the Académie Suisse or learned traditional painting and drawing at the official École des Beaux-Arts. Degas was a student there and first met Manet while copying a painting at the Louvre Museum.

Édouard Manet was an important figure in the shift from realism to impressionism.

Studio in the Rue La Condamine, Frédéric Bazille, 1870

Bazille's Studio

At Gleyre's studio, Monet, Renoir, and Sisley befriended Frédéric Bazille. This talented young painter came from a wealthy family and often helped the others out financially. The image at left shows the studio he shared with Renoir (seated far left). You can also see Zola (on the stairs) and Monet, Bazille himself, and Manet by the easel.

A Garden Gathering

Manet's paintings of contemporary life were fresh, untraditional, and thrilling to the impressionists. In *Music in the Tuileries* (below), Manet shows himself (far left) among a crowd at an outdoor concert. It's a noisy, bustling scene with scattered splashes of bright color. While some figures are painted in detail, others are only loosely sketched in.

Music in the Tuileries, Édouard Manet, 1862

Look Closer

Manet painted a seething mass of people. How does he make certain figures stand out? Look at his use of light and dark and the way everything is arranged on the canvas. Does the scene look 3D or flat?

"I paint what I see and not what others like to see."

Manet

Open-Air Art

Learning in the studio was one thing, but for the impressionists the open air called. From 1863 they made regular trips to the Fontainebleau forest, about an hour from Paris by train. Here they set up their easels and painted outdoors.

The Barbizon School

Open-air, or *plein-air*, painting was nothing new in the 19th century. Many artists made sketches out in the countryside, though they usually finished their work indoors. In the 1830s a group including Camille Corot (right) and Théodore Rousseau made outdoor painting a trend. Named the Barbizon School after a village near Fontainebleau, they inspired the impressionists by painting vividly colored scenes at different times of day.

Portable Painting

Plein-air artists were grateful for the invention of screw-cap paint tubes in 1841. Before that oil paints were stored in pouches made from pigs' bladders, and they dried out quickly once they were opened. New portable easels also made life easier when it came to carrying equipment across the countryside.

Fontainebleau: Oak Trees at Bas-Bréau,
Camille Corot, 1832–1833

Why Paint Outdoors?

Outdoor painting helped the impressionists to be spontaneous. If they were standing in a forest and a gust of wind caught the trees, they could paint it! When a cloud passed the sun or the evening shadows lengthened, they could capture the changing colors in that moment. None of this was possible in an enclosed studio with unwavering artificial light.

Hermitage at Pontoise, Camille Pissarro, about 1867

A Village Scene

Camille Pissarro painted the scene above near Pontoise, northwest of Paris. You can see his interest in the effects of sunlight and shade on the gleaming path and hedges. He also included some ordinary villagers—people rarely seen in art before the realists. Figures like this often punctuate Pissarro's landscapes.

⋯⋯→ Look Closer

The impressionists learned from the Barbizon artists, working repeatedly in the same place to capture different light and weather. What time of day do you think it is in the painting above?

On the Beach

You can almost feel the whispering sea breeze and the heat of the sun on the sand. In this atmospheric painting, Monet swept up the sensations of being at the beach and put them down on canvas.

The Beach at Trouville, Claude Monet, 1870

Sand in the Paint

It was the summer of 1870, and Monet was on vacation in the French resort of Trouville with his new wife Camille, shown on the left of the painting above. Imagine the artist on the breezy beach, brushes in hand and fresh colors on his palette—it's no wonder that when you look closely at this canvas, you can see grains of sand in the paint!

Fast Work

Monet worked quickly to express the fleeting conditions of the seaside. He slapped bold streaks of white across Camille's lap, showing where the sunlight caught her skirt. Neither her face nor her companion's is shown in any detail. This incomplete finish is typical of impressionism—it reminds us how changing light can blur the edges of things.

Inspiring Artist

Monet and Camille were visiting an old friend, the artist Eugène Boudin. It was Boudin who had introduced the teenage Monet to outdoor painting, taking him on expeditions around the Normandy coast. Boudin encouraged Monet to "see the light" and observe the changing weather. His own paintings show glimpses of the broken brushwork that became a hallmark of impressionism.

"Three brushstrokes from nature are worth more than two days in the studio."
Eugène Boudin

The Beach at Trouville, Eugène Boudin, 1865

Look Closer

Compare Monet's and Boudin's paintings. What similarities can you see? What are the differences? Think about the colors, composition, and brushstrokes.

Fleeing War

While the Monets were in Trouville, the Franco-Prussian War broke out in eastern France. Monet, Pissarro, and Sisley all fled to England to escape the fighting. While there, they continued to paint and admired work by British artists such as John Constable and J.M.W. Turner. Meanwhile, their friend Bazille sadly died in battle.

Breaking Boundaries

Most artists working when the impressionists started out pinned their hopes on the Paris Salon. This important exhibition, held every year or so, was one of the few ways they could gain recognition. Unfortunately, not everyone made the grade.

Salon Standards

The Salon jury had strict standards set by the Académie des Beaux-Arts. They favored realistic but idealized images, usually with religious or classical themes like this Delaroche painting at right, set in ancient Greece. They expected skillful drawing, delicate shading, use of perspective, and a flawless finish. Although there were exceptions to these academic rules, anything radically different was rejected.

Hémicycle (section 2), Paul Delaroche, 1841–1842

Man with a Hoe, Jean-François Millet, 1860–1862

Look Closer

Realists like Jean-François Millet criticized the "false" perfection of academic art. Look at the differences between Millet's painting and Delaroche's. *Man with a Hoe* (above) was accepted by the Salon in 1863—but it caused controversy. Can you see why?

The Exhibition of Rejected Art

In 1863 the Salon refused nearly 3,000 of 5,000 works! These included paintings by Manet, Pissarro, and Degas. When the ruling Emperor Napoleon III found out, he decided to stage a "rejected art" exhibition—the Salon des Refusés. It attracted more than a thousand visitors a day, many of whom came to laugh.

A Very Modern Picnic

By far the most talked-about Refusés painting was Manet's *Luncheon On the Grass* (below). It showed a naked woman sharing a picnic with modern men—a shocking departure from biblical or mythical nudes. Equally rebellious was Manet's use of light, with garish contrasts instead of subtle shading. His scene also lacked perspective—the traditional way of painting depth and distance.

Luncheon on the Grass, Édouard Manet, 1863

New Independence

Napoleon did not like Manet's painting. He called it "an offence to dignity" and regretted the Salon des Refusés. Nonetheless, the exhibition had a vital impact. It highlighted the gap between traditional art and new ideas, and it loosened the grip of the official Salon. Artists felt more freedom to display their paintings independently.

Impressions Rising

In the spring of 1874, 30 artists took a gamble. They boycotted the Salon and instead exhibited their art in a former photography studio. The show was hardly a massive hit—but it did earn the group a name.

First Impressions

Monet's *Impression, Sunrise* (below) was just one of 165 works in the exhibition. When the critic Louis Leroy saw the painting, he said it looked like unfinished wallpaper! He called his review "Exhibition of the Impressionists," meaning this as an insult, as "real" artists did not paint mere impressions. A few years later, the artists were using the name "impressionist" themselves.

Sketchy Sunrise

You can see why Monet chose the title *Impression, Sunrise.* His painting shows a suggestion, or an idea, of a place. It gives us the feeling of a warm sun rising over water without fully describing where it is. The sketchy brushwork implies that the scene is not static, but always changing. At any moment, a boat will cut across the blazing orange reflection.

Impression, Sunrise, Claude Monet, 1872

An Intimate Moment

The only female artist to exhibit in the 1874 show was Berthe Morisot. Her painting *The Cradle* (below) shows her sister Edma watching over her sleeping baby. Although the subject is a long way from Monet's, the essence of a moment in time is the same. It is an intimate snapshot, stumbled upon by the painter.

Art for Art's Sake

One thing that's clear from these two paintings is just that—they are paintings! The artists weren't trying to trick the viewer by creating an illusion of the real world. They didn't hide their brush marks, and they depicted personal experiences rather than grand ideas. This "art for art's sake" marked a big break from traditional painting.

The Cradle, Berthe Morisot, 1872

Look Closer

There's an amazing sense of quiet in this painting. How has Morisot emphasized the private moment between a mother and her baby?

A Color Revolution

The impressionists veered toward bright, pure colors that surprised people used to traditional art. But there was science behind the artists' thinking, and they learned from painters of the past too.

Simultaneous Contrast

In the 1830s a chemist named Michel Eugène Chevreul devised a wheel showing how colors relate to one another. He observed that red, for example, looks at its most intense when placed next to its opposite, or complementary, color green. This "simultaneous contrast," as he called it, was a magical discovery for the impressionists.

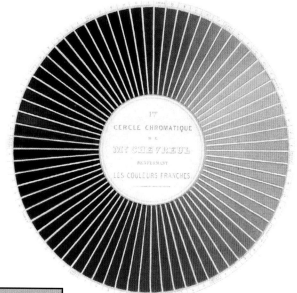

The Effect of Snow at Argenteuil, Alfred Sisley, 1874

Sunlight and Shadows

How much plain white can you see in this snowy scene at left? In fact, there is very little. Although we think of snow as white, it changes with the light. Sisley sprinkled it with sunny yellow and added shadows in complementary violet and blue. Blue and violet shadows were so popular with the impressionists that critics said they had "indigomania!"

Banning Brown

The Romantic artist Eugène Delacroix (1798–1863) was an early fan of Chevreul's theories. He decided to banish black and traditional earth hues (browns and ochres) from his palette. To darken colors, he mixed in their complementaries; to lighten them he added white. The impressionists took these ideas on board.

New Paints

Thanks to developments in paint technology, the impressionists had a wide range of pigments to choose from. Vivid new colors like cerulean blue appeared in the mid-1800s, and synthetic versions of traditional hues, such as ultramarine, became more affordable. To make their colors as vibrant as possible, the impressionists usually painted on a white background.

"No shadow is black. It always has a color.
Nature knows only colors. . . ."

Renoir

The Artist's Palette with a Landscape, Camille Pissarro, about 1878

A Palette Painting

To make his point about color, Pissarro painted the scene above on a palette! Around the edge, he left blobs of the only six paints he used. Notice how there are no earth hues. You can see the use of white and yellow to brighten sunlit grass, while the shadows are darkened with crimson and blue.

An Exciting City

Huge, grand boulevards, rumbling with horse-drawn carriages; fashionable people strolling in tree-lined parks; noisy bars and cafés; glamorous theaters. Paris at the time of the impressionists was an exciting place to be.

Modern Makeover

Napoleon III transformed the French capital in the 1850s and 1860s from medieval city to modern metropolis. The architect Baron Haussman was in charge of this impressive makeover. The Industrial Revolution, recently arrived in France, had brought more people to the cities to work in factories, shops, and offices. They had more leisure time than rural workers—and more money to spend on it.

Paris Street; Rainy Day, Gustave Caillebotte, 1877

Boulevard des Capucines, Claude Monet, 1873

Paris in the Rain

The above painting by Gustave Caillebotte highlights just how monumental Haussman's streets seemed. The figures look small and strangely still within the gigantic space. Everything in the picture appears ordered and immaculate— until you notice the clash of umbrellas that might happen any moment in the right-hand corner!

Look Closer ◄ ┄┄┄┄┄┄┄┄┄┄┄┄┄┄┄┄

Monet painted Paris in a very different way. What differences do you notice between the painting above and Caillebotte's scene? Which do you think best captures the city's energy?

Ball at the Moulin de la Galette,
Pierre-Auguste Renoir, 1876

Dancing Days

Dances in Montmartre were a popular way for Parisians to spend a Sunday afternoon. Renoir caught the happy atmosphere in the dizzying, sun-dappled painting above. He persuaded his friends to pose with local working girls, gossiping and twirling under the trees. It looks like a flurry of fun and relaxation, but Renoir has arranged everything carefully to balance the colors and shapes.

River Scenes

While the hubbub of Paris captivated the impressionists, they also spent time in quieter suburbs along the Seine River. Many of them painted at the yachting center of Argenteuil, where Monet settled for much of the 1870s.

Studio Boat

To really get to know the river, Monet converted a boat into a floating studio. Often he anchored it close to other boats so he could study their reflections in the water. When Manet came to visit in 1874, he painted Monet painting (right)! The swish of his brushstrokes echoes the rock of the boat.

Monet on his Studio Boat, Édouard Manet, 1874

Boat in the Flood, Port Marly, Alfred Sisley, 1876

Calm After the Flood

In 1876 part of the Seine burst its banks at the village of Port Marly. Sisley rushed to paint there, capturing the floodwater as it washed over buildings and trees. The bright blue sky takes up much of his canvas (right) and is reflected in the river below. Although there is a ripple of movement in the water, the scene feels tranquil and quiet.

Night on the Thames

In England another artist was painting mesmerizing views of water—this time the Thames River. American painter James McNeill Whistler had studied in Paris and befriended Monet in London. Whistler washed his panels with thin layers of paint, rather than chunky splashes. But he was seeking to unravel the secrets of light and atmosphere, just as the impressionists were.

Nocturne: Blue and Gold, Old Battersea Bridge, James McNeill Whistler, 1872–1875

〰▶ *Look Closer*

Monet greatly admired Whistler's work. Can you see similarities between this *Nocturne* (above) and Monet's *Impression, Sunrise* on page 14?

Wonderful Water

The impressionists returned time and time again to painting water and reflections. There was no better subject for getting to grips with the ever-changing effects of light. As well as rivers, they painted the sea in all states from calm to stormy. Monet loved the sea so much that he joked he wanted to be buried in a buoy!

In Focus: Double Vision

One view . . . two painters . . . two visions! Camille Pissarro and Paul Cézanne spent many days in the 1870s working side by side outdoors. These two pictures were painted independently, but they seem to show a similar place.

So Alike . . .

The likeness between the works on these two pages is quite striking. They both show a thicket of tall, thin trees towering over a cluster of houses. The trees rise up in the middle ground of each scene and are cut off by the top of the canvas. Everything is perched on a steep, rugged slope with a path winding across the left-hand corner.

Yet So Different

Now notice the differences! See how Pissarro's canvas is densely covered with a thatch of small marks. They almost merge together in front of our eyes, unlike Cézanne's broad strokes of paint. Cézanne's colors are warm and bright, while Pissarro's look cooler, more shady. Another subtle difference is Pissarro's inclusion of two figures.

Pissarro's Pontoise

Pissarro was living in Pontoise at this point, and he loved this leafy spot in the nearby hills. The human element of his scene makes it inviting, despite the spiky tangle of trees. Although he used thick paint, or *impasto*, his marks seem to skip lightly across the canvas. Our eye naturally follows the lines of the branches up to the airy sky, top right.

The Côte des Boeufs at L'Hermitage, Camille Pissarro, 1877

22

Cézanne's Solid Shapes

Cézanne worked slowly and deliberately. He shared a lot with the impressionists, but he also wanted to show the solid side of nature beneath the changing light. His marks are carefully organized, treated the same in the background as they are in the foreground. This flat, blocky style inspired later artists and led to an art movement called cubism.

Orchard, Côte St-Denis at Pontoise, Paul Cézanne, 1877

Look Closer

A villager who once watched these artists paint
said that Pissarro dabbed while Cézanne daubed!
Whose brushwork do you prefer, and why?

23

The Age of Steam

Imagine the thrill of a loud, puffing steam engine roaring toward you when you'd never seen a train before! The French railway network grew up during the impressionists' lifetime, and it captured their imagination as a symbol of the modern age.

All Change!

Trains transformed people's lives, carrying workers into Paris from the suburbs and back out of town for country weekends. Not only did the impressionists take advantage of train travel, but they also delighted in the play of shiny, industrial railways with the landscape. This subject matter was new and not to many people's taste at the time.

A Gentle Journey

Pissarro painted the train below when he was in London during the Franco-Prussian War. Unusually for him, there are no people in the scene, just a locomotive chugging along a track. It looks natural in its surroundings, softly painted and leaving a gentle trail of steam. Even though as viewers we are directly in its path, there is nothing threatening about it.

Lordship Lane Station, Dulwich, Camille Pissarro, 1871

Busy at the Station

Monet loved the way steam seemed to muffle and dissolve solid structures. He worked so often at the Gare Saint-Lazare in Paris that the stationmaster would move trains for him or even puff out steam on demand! At right is one of 12 views he painted of the station, each time capturing a different angle or light effect. He showed seven of them at the Third Impressionist Exhibition in 1877.

Gare Saint-Lazare, Claude Monet, 1877

Speeding Ahead

Both Pissarro and Monet had seen the work of J.M.W. Turner in London. Turner's *Rain, Steam and Speed* (below) is a dramatic interpretation of a train hurtling over the Thames River. We can feel a sense of danger from the fast pace of the vehicle. This would have been incredible for people who had only traveled on foot, on horseback, or by horse and carriage before.

Rain, Steam and Speed—The Great Western Railway, J.M.W. Turner, 1844

Look Closer

Turner's atmospheric style inspired the impressionists. Can you see similarities in their work? How has Turner created the sense of speed above? Look at the way he applied the paint.

Life Through the Lens

In today's world where photography is everywhere, it is hard not to take it for granted. But when the first shutter clicked in the 19th century, it was a very big deal. Photography revolutionized art—and the impressionists used it to their advantage.

Beyond Real

By the late 1870s, photography had been around for over 30 years. Cameras weren't yet available to everyone, but photographers could record scenes and people in an instant. Some artists worried that this would take over from painting. But the impressionists saw it as a ticket to experiment—if a photo could accurately depict the real world, then they didn't need to!

Snapshot Style

Snapshot photographs particularly intrigued the impressionists. They noticed how, in these unposed pictures, figures and objects were often cropped off at the edge. Sometimes people stepped right in front of the camera, upsetting the composition. And if anything within the picture moved, it came out as a blur. Why not put all this in paint?

Horse Galloping, Eadweard Muybridge, 1878

Horses in Motion

Degas was fascinated by photography. He studied the work of Eadweard Muybridge, who took sequences of photos exploring movement and freezing it in time (left). You can see the influence of Muybridge in the poses of Degas' racehorse painting at right. Notice too how the scene is like a spontaneous snapshot, with horses and a carriage moving in and out of the frame.

At the Races, Edgar Degas, about 1877–1880

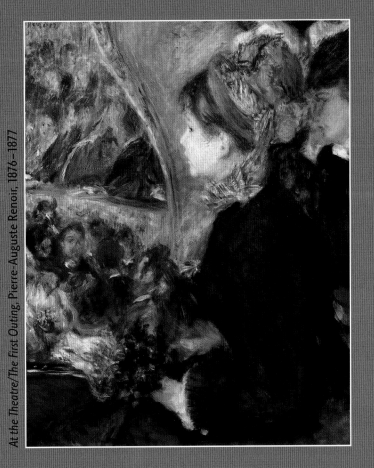

At the Theatre/The First Outing, Pierre-Auguste Renoir, 1876–1877

Watching the Audience

Photography captured real people in real time—the present, not the past. This appealed to the impressionists. Renoir also loved the idea of watching people watching, like this painting at right of an audience at the theater. Only the foreground figure is in focus, while the rest is blurred in a hum of motion. As a painter, Renoir could also add something that early cameras couldn't—color.

⋯⋯⋯▶ *Look Closer*

Look at the paintings throughout this book—can you see the influence of photography? What features show this?

Dancing with Degas

In a world of her own, a graceful ballerina shimmers like a star on the stage. Her movement seems effortless, although we know her muscles are straining. Edgar Degas compared ballet to his own art—it took a lot of hard work to make something look this easy!

High Viewpoint

Degas painted this dancer (right) from a high viewpoint, as if watching her from a theater box. Her body is foreshortened as she tilts toward us, and one leg is out of sight. Degas liked to remind us how our field of vision is limited—we can see only certain parts of things from certain angles. His interest in photography and the cropping of the camera is clear here too.

On the Sidelines

Notice all the bare floor in this picture! Instead of placing the star in the center, Degas has pushed her to one side. Behind her, figures wait in the wings, their heads chopped off by pieces of scenery. This quirky composition shows the influence of Japanese prints.

Edgar Degas in 1917

Ballet Mania

Degas was obsessed with the ballet. He said what he liked most was painting movement and pretty clothes. Throughout his career, he drew and painted dancers—sometimes on stage, but more often rehearsing, stretching, rubbing aching muscles, or tying shoes behind the scenes. As well as sketching at the theater, he regularly paid girls to pose for him in his studio.

The Star, Edgar Degas, 1878

Delicate Star

Degas used pastels to capture the dancer's delicate dress and the glow of her skin under the spotlight. The rippling black ribbons and the direction of his marks make her seem to move. She is as light as a feather, in contrast with the dark, heavy strokes of the background. Everything is angled so that our gaze is drawn toward her.

Women's Worlds

Behind all the hustle and bustle of the modern world, most impressionists also painted domestic moments. They portrayed family and friends in their gardens and homes—especially the female artists who had less freedom socially.

Female Artists

Becoming an artist was difficult for women in the 19th century. Respectable ladies were expected to stay at home or keep polite female company—they couldn't paint on the streets or in bars and cafés like male artists did. To pay for art lessons, they also needed to come from a wealthy family.

Modern Interiors

American painter Mary Cassatt was excited when Degas invited her to join the impressionists in 1877. She was producing works as modern as theirs, and she and Morisot became as important to the movement as their male friends. Cassatt painted well-dressed women drinking tea, at the theater, or looking after children. But her paintings were more rebellious than that sounds.

Little Girl in a Blue Armchair, Mary Cassatt, 1878

Armchair Attitude

Look at the attitude in this above painting of a girl slumped casually in an armchair. Although she is in elegant surroundings, there is nothing prim and proper about her pose. She seems bored and out of place in the grown-up room—which is probably exactly how she felt. Cassatt abandoned the idea of refined behavior and painted something more honest.

Summer's Day, Berthe Morisot, 1879

An Elegant Outing

Berthe Morisot exhibited with the impressionists from 1874 onward. She knew
Manet and Degas well and married Manet's brother. Her work is easy to identify
through its sweeping brushwork, which swishes confidently across the canvas.
To paint this outing on a lake in the Bois de Bologne (above), she sat in the
same boat as her two models.

Look Closer

Morisot's brushstrokes zigzag back and forth, creating a
gentle sense of motion. Notice how there are very few
outlines in the painting. What effect does this have?

In Focus: Painting a Party

The sun is shining and a group of friends relax on the balcony of a restaurant. Lunch is almost over, but they're in no hurry to leave. Renoir spent months changing and rearranging the figures this painting, many of whom are his own friends.

Pierre-Auguste Renoir

Best in Show

When *Luncheon of the Boating Party* (right) appeared in the Seventh Impressionist Exhibition, it wowed the critics. They loved the sumptuous colors, the happy atmosphere, and the artful posing of the figures. Renoir cleverly bounced light around the scene, using bright white in the tablecloth, the sleeveless shirts, and the suited men's collars. He worked with feathery strokes that seem to give life to the paint.

What's Happening?

What are these people in the painting talking about? Why are they here? The answer is, we have no idea! Renoir didn't try to tell a story with his picture—he was more interested in pleasing our eyes. This is one important thing that made impressionism different from art that came before it. These works were informal and didn't commemorate anything.

Modern Society

What the painting does show is how French society was changing. Though class divisions still existed, they were starting to break down to form a new middle-class bourgeoisie. The characters here are a diverse mix of artists, writers, bureaucrats, actresses, and shop girls. They are all chatting openly, uninhibited by their different walks of life.

Traditional Traits

Renoir soaked up many influences, including Old Masters such as Peter Paul Rubens (1577–1640), who was known for his clever grouping of figures. The way Renoir used light and shade here to model his characters also reflects his interest in traditional art. This scene has more depth than some of his earlier works, with the river receding into the distance. Meanwhile, the fruit and glasses on the table resemble a still life.

Luncheon of the Boating Party, Pierre-Auguste Renoir, 1880–1881

"... We have freed painting from the subject.
I can paint flowers and simply call them
'flowers' without their having a story."
Renoir

The Craze for Japan

When Japan opened its ports in the second half of the 19th century, a craze for all things oriental struck Europe. The impressionists were quick to join in, collecting Japanese prints and borrowing elements of their style.

New Trade

Japan had long been closed to the western world—but new trade agreements in the 1850s brought a flood of Japanese art, fans, fashions, and other goods to Europe. Woodblock prints known as *ukiyo-e* particularly caught the eye of the impressionists.

Floating Worlds

Ukiyo-e, or "pictures of the floating world," looked nothing like European art. They often showed scenes from unusually high viewpoints or cropped off, much like snapshots. There was little concern for depth or perspective, but instead flat colors and asymmetrical compositions dominated. Needless to say, the impressionists loved these daring features.

Young Man Playing a Flute, Tanaka Masunobu, about 1740–1750

Pillar Pictures

Degas was inspired by a Japanese print format in this drawing of Mary Cassatt at right. *Hashira-e*, or pillar pictures (left), were tall and narrow—challenging to fit a full image in. The artists cropped their figures at the sides and often stacked them one above another. Degas imitated this by partly hiding his two ladies behind a wall.

Look Closer

The people in the Japanese woodblock prints (left) are wearing kimonos. Can you see how Degas mimics their shapes in his painting? What do you notice about the viewpoint in these works, and the angle of lines in the background?

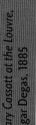

Mary Cassatt at the Louvre,
Edgar Degas, 1885

Woman Bathing, Mary Cassatt, about 1891

Imitation Prints

Degas, Cassatt, and Pissarro all experimented with printmaking, though they etched their designs into metal plates rather than wooden blocks. The decorative feel of Cassatt's *Woman Bathing* (left) is typically Japanese. She used clean lines and flat colors with no shadows, just like *ukiyo-e*. Female figures in domestic settings were also well-known subjects in Japanese art.

A Determined Dealer

At first, the impressionists had trouble convincing people to buy their radical work. But after many years of financial hardship, their fortunes started to change. A lot of this came down to one forward-thinking man—the art dealer Paul Durand-Ruel.

Paul Durand-Ruel

Experimental Eye

Durand-Ruel met Monet and Pissarro in London in 1870 and soon got to know their impressionist friends. The artists were amazed that this man willingly bought their pictures—and for the asking price too! Durand-Ruel had an eye for experimental works, and he was determined to change the public's mind about the impressionists.

A Struggle to Sell

Representing modern artists was not easy. People in traditional art circles thought Durand-Ruel was mad! At times he came close to bankruptcy because he couldn't sell the impressionist works he had bought. But he carried on staging exhibitions for his artists—in Berlin, London, and other cities, as well as at home in Paris—and eventually his hard work paid off.

Creative Marketing

Durand-Ruel had innovative ways of marketing his artists. He held unprecedented solo shows, produced engravings of their works, and even printed them in a set along with paintings by established artists. He encouraged them to try commercial formats, like this fan painting by Pissarro (below). In addition, he supported the impressionists with loans and studio space when they could barely afford to buy paints.

The Harvesters,
Camille Pissarro, about 1880

Success!

The turning point came in 1886, when Durand-Ruel held an impressionist exhibition in New York. He already had a good reputation there, having successfully shown works from the Barbizon School years before. The impressionists were a hit with the American audience—almost every painting sold! Paris soon took note, and at last the radical artists triumphed.

"We would have died of hunger without Durand-Ruel. . . . We owe him everything."
Monet

New Impressions

Just weeks after Durand-Ruel launched the impressionists in the United States, they held their eighth and last group show in Paris. By now the artists were beginning to go their separate ways, and new styles were emerging.

The Final Show

Only Pissarro showed work in all eight impressionist exhibitions. The others came and went, holding solo shows or repeatedly trying their luck at the Salon. In this final exhibition of 1886, Monet, Morisot, Cassatt, and others were reunited—and some new faces put in an appearance too.

Joining the Dots

The work that attracted the most attention was an enormous canvas smothered in dots! The below painting by Georges Seurat was the showcase of a new style, neo-impressionism. Instead of mixing paints on a palette, Seurat let our eyes do the work. He carefully arranged tiny "points" of pure color so that they seemed to merge together. This technique became known as pointillism.

A Sunday Afternoon on the Island of La Grande Jatte,
Georges Seurat, 1884–1886

Showing Emotion

Other artists had different ambitions. Paul Gauguin and Vincent van Gogh wanted their work to show emotion, not just the physical world. Rather than simply copying nature, they used their memories and imaginations too. Gauguin painted with flat color and line, while van Gogh used expressive brushstrokes. These artists and others of the same time period became known as post-impressionists.

An Agitated Mood

Van Gogh painted this dreamlike scene below while he was suffering from mental health problems. You can see the influence of the impressionists' broken brushstrokes, but these swirling marks are loaded with feeling. We get a sense of agitation and loneliness but also hope in the bright stars. Capturing moods, either of the artist or of the subject, became an increasing feature in modern art.

The Starry Night, Vincent van Gogh, 1889

Patterns on a Pond

Flowers, leaves, and watery reflections span a huge canvas edge to edge. We can't tell if this is a small pond or a huge lake—there's no sign of where it begins and ends! Monet took a giant leap from giving scenes a context when he painted his series of water lilies.

Water Lilies, Claude Monet, 1906

New Directions

Late in life, many of the impressionists took their work in new directions. Degas and Renoir focused on figures, Pissarro experimented with neo-impressionism, and Monet became more concerned with color and light than the subject itself. Whether it was haystacks, cathedrals, or his pond at Giverny, he painted things over and over again in changing conditions.

The Giverny Garden

Monet moved to Giverny in the 1880s and later bought a house where he would build a beloved Japanese-style garden. He produced close to 250 water lily paintings here, as well as other views of the pond and foliage. Exploring the garden's natural colors and textures occupied the last 30 years of his life.

All Ends Up

In a way, Monet was turning art upside down when he painted his water lilies—looking down at his garden pond, flipping its horizontal surface on to a vertical canvas. There is no horizon line and no sense of distance, so our eyes have nowhere to go but around the picture surface. This brave new focus on the paint itself was an inspiration to later abstract artists.

Gigantic Panels

From 1914 Monet painted a series of vast, panoramic water lily panels (below). He had to build a special glass-roofed studio and prop his canvases on wheels to move them around. Eight of the panels now decorate two rooms at the Orangerie Museum in Paris. Just as Monet intended, when you stand among them it is like being plunged into an endless watery world.

Look Closer

Monet built up rich, decorative patterns with his paint. Can you see how this inspired artists like Jackson Pollock (1912–1956) on page 45? How is Pollock's work different?

World Impressions

During the later years of impressionism, artists abroad began catching on to the style. They saw exhibitions in their own countries or traveled to France to study. Other art forms, from film to literature, were also influenced by the movement.

Inspiring Europe

Many of the impressionists traveled in the 1880s and 1890s around France, Europe, and even North Africa. They picked up friends and influences along the way and held exhibitions abroad. Artists they inspired included Germany's Max Liebermann, Italy's Giuseppi de Nittis, and England's Philip Wilson Steer.

Boulogne Sands, Philip Wilson Steer, 1888–1891

Wedding March, Theodore Robinson, 1892

American Enthusiasm

American artists, encouraged by Cassatt and Durand-Ruel, were quick to flock to France for inspiration. Theodore Robinson was one of the first to visit Monet in Giverny, where a colony of foreign artists soon grew up. Back home, Robinson and others spread the word and American impressionism thrived until around 1913 when new trends in modern art emerged.

▶ *Look Closer*

This painting above by Theodore Robinson shows the wedding of Monet's stepdaughter to an American artist. How is it similar to French impressionist works?

The Heidelberg School

Impressionism even reached as far afield as Australia! Led by Tom Roberts, who had visited France, a group of artists known as the Heidelberg School painted the effects of light on their vast landscape. In 1889 they held a "9 by 5 Impressionist Exhibition." Most of the paintings, including the one below by Charles Conder, were done on cigar box panels, just 9 by 5 inches (23 x 13 centimeters) in size.

Centennial Choir at Sorrento, Charles Conder, 1889

Beyond Painting

Renoir's son Jean was a filmmaker. From the 1920s he directed an impressionist style of cinema with artistic shots resembling the paintings of his father and friends. Musicians such as Claude Debussy wrote atmospheric compositions that were linked to impressionism too. Even writers, including Joseph Conrad and Virginia Woolf, began hinting at, rather than fully describing scenes.

Making Art Modern

By the end of their lives, the impressionists' distinctive style was finally appreciated. Not only that, but it helped to shape the art of the future. A new generation of artists took advantage of the freedom the impressionists had created, and modern art was born.

Mont Saint-Victoire, Paul Cézanne, 1902–1904

Cézanne and Cubism

Paul Cézanne has been called both an impressionist and a post-impressionist, but he also paved the way for cubist artists like Pablo Picasso (1881–1973). You can see in the painting at left how Cézanne's blocky technique became increasingly exaggerated as time went by. The way he saw nature as a series of geometric shapes inspired the cubists to simplify and flatten forms yet further.

Away from Nature

Some early 20th century painters, including Henri Matisse, took the impressionists' bright colors to a new extreme known as fauvism. Others, such as Pierre Bonnard, produced decorative paintings with similar brushwork to the impressionists. In both of these cases, as well as with the cubists, art moved further from being representational.

Renewed Interest

Pure impressionism went out of fashion while the new waves of modern art took the limelight. But in the 1950s, a movement called abstract expressionism emerged in the United States. The colorful, textural images by artists such as Jackson Pollock (right) reminded people of Monet's water lilies and other works. It was time to exhibit impressionist paintings again—and they caused a sensation.

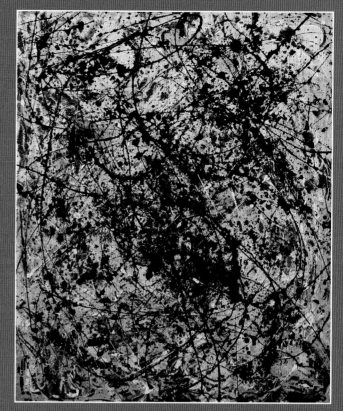

Reflection of the Big Dipper, Jackson Pollock, 1947

Overwhelming Success

Today impressionist scenes are the ultimate crowd pleasers, seen on calendars, mouse pads, toiletry bags, and more! People can relate to the everyday subjects, the shimmering colors, and the contemplative moods. When Roy Lichtenstein (1923–1997) created *Rouen Cathedral, Set 5*, based on a series of paintings by Monet, he was commenting on the way we mass-reproduce impressionist works. The popularity and merchandising we see today would have been unimaginable when these artists were alive.

Rouen Cathedral, Set 5, Roy Lichtenstein, 1969

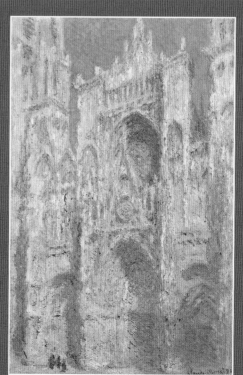

Rouen Cathedral, Claude Monet, 1894

Glossary

abstract—not representing an actual object, place, or living thing; abstract art often focuses on basic shapes, lines and colors

abstract expressionism—an American art style (1940s–1950s) based on creating art for emotional effect, rather than representing something physical

academic art—art based on the principles of the French Academy of Fine Arts (Académie des Beaux-Arts)

asymmetrical—lop-sided

avant-garde—new and experimental

boulevard—a wide street

canvas—a strong type of fabric that many artists use to paint on

classical—relating to ancient Greek and Roman culture, which influenced breakthroughs in art during the Renaissance (1350–1550)

colony—a community of people settling in a foreign place

complementary colors—colors that have maximum contrast between each other; the basic pairs for artists are red and green, blue and orange, and yellow and purple

composition—the way parts of a picture or sculpture are arranged

cubists—artists led by Pablo Picasso and Georges Braque, who made images using geometric shapes and multiple viewpoints (1907–1920s)

engraving—a print made from an engraved design

etch—to engrave a design, usually on a metal plate for printing

fauvism—an art movement (1905–1910) in which artists such as Henri Matisse used extreme colors and fierce brushstrokes

foreshorten—to paint something shorter than it really is, so it appears to be receding into space

Franco-Prussian War—a conflict from 1870 to 1871 between France and north German states, led by the kingdom of Prussia

idealized—made to look more perfect than reality

illusion—something that tricks the eye or isn't what it seems

impasto—using paint thickly so that it stands out from the picture surface

Industrial Revolution—the rapid development in industry and mechanization that began in around 1760

medieval—relating to the Middle Ages, the period from about 500 to the 1450s

palette—a board that artists mix their paints on; also used to describe the range of colors in a painting

perspective—the art of showing three-dimensional objects on a flat surface, creating the effect of depth and distance

pigment—a type of coloring, usually in powdered form, that forms the basis of paint

representational—showing the true physical appearance of things

sketch—a rough drawing, done in preparation for a finished work

still life—a painting or drawing of an arrangement of objects, such as fruit in a bowl or flowers in a vase

studio—an artist's indoor workplace

synthetic—artificially or chemically made, usually to imitate a natural product

texture—the feel of a surface, such as rough brick or smooth glass

woodcut print—a print made by carving a design into a block of wood, covering it in paint or ink and pressing it onto a surface

Read More

Books

Gunderson, Jessica. *Impressionism*. Odysseys in Art. Mankato, Minn.: Creative Education, 2016.

Wood, Alix. *Impressionist Art*. Create It! New York: Gareth Stevens, 2017.

Internet Sites

Impressionism: Art of Impressionists
www.impressionism.org

The Metropolitan Museum of Art: Impressionism: Art and Modernity
www.metmuseum.org/toah/hd/imml/hd_imml.htm

National Gallery of Art: Impressionism
www.nga.gov/features/slideshows/impressionism.html

The Art Story: Impressionism
www.theartstory.org/movement-impressionism.htm

Timeline

1830s Artists of the Barbizon School pioneer outdoor, or *plein-air*, painting.

1841 Screw-cap metal paint tubes are invented, making oil paints portable and reusable.

1850s French realists begin painting ordinary people working the land.

1852 Napoleon III launches his plans to modernize Paris, including grand new boulevards and railways.

1855 Degas enrolls at the École des Beaux-Arts in Paris. Pissarro also studies there, as well as at the Académie Suisse.

about 1856 Monet meets Boudin, who encourages him to work in the open air.

1859 Monet moves to Paris and meets Pissarro at the Académie Suisse.

1860s The craze for Japanese prints begins in France, influencing the emerging impressionists.

1861 Cézanne moves to Paris, where he meets Monet and Pissarro.

1862 Monet enters Charles Gleyre's studio and meets Renoir, Sisley, and Bazille. Manet paints *Music in the Tuileries* and meets Degas at the Louvre.

1863 Monet leads expeditions to paint outdoors in the Fontainebleau forest. The Salon des Refusés is held, causing a scandal with Manet's *Luncheon on the Grass*.

1866 Cassatt moves from the United States to Paris.

1868 Manet meets Morisot at the Louvre.

1869 Monet and Renoir paint some of the first true impressionist works at La Grenouillère, on the banks of the Seine River.

1870 The Franco-Prussian War breaks out. Monet and Pissarro flee to England, where they discover work by Turner and meet the art dealer Durand-Ruel.

1871 The war ends. Monet and Pissarro return to France, where Monet settles at Argenteuil.

1872 Pissarro settles in Pontoise, where he introduces Cézanne to outdoor painting.

1873 Monet meets Caillebotte.

1874 The First Impressionist Exhibition takes place in the studio of a photographer called Nadar. Based on Monet's *Impression, Sunrise*, a critic coins the term "impressionist."

1876 The Second Impressionist Exhibition is held at Durand-Ruel's gallery.

1877 The Third Impressionist Exhibition includes seven of Monet's *Gare St-Lazare* paintings.

1877-1878 Muybridge takes his pioneering photographs of horses in motion, inspiring Degas.

1879 Cassatt shows work in the Fourth Impressionist Exhibition.

1880 At the Fifth Impressionist Exhibition, several major names including Monet are missing.

1881 The Sixth Impressionist Exhibition shows further dispersal of the group. Monet, Renoir, Sisley, and Manet all exhibit at the Salon.

1882 Monet, Renoir, and Sisley join in again at the Seventh Impressionist Exhibition. Renoir receives high praise for his *Luncheon of the Boating Party*.

1883 Monet moves to Giverny, northwest of Paris.

1885 Pissarro meets Seurat and begins to experiment with neo-impressionism. Tom Roberts forms the Heidelberg School in Australia.

1886 Seurat attracts attention at the Eighth Impressionist Exhibition. Gauguin also shows his work, and meets van Gogh who moves to Paris in the same year. Durand-Ruel holds an impressionist exhibition in New York.

1892 U.S. artist Theodore Robinson returns home from Giverny and helps to grow the American impressionist movement.

1899 Monet begins his series of water lily paintings.

1903 Pissarro dies in Paris.

1906 Cézanne dies in Provence.

1907 Picasso and Braque make the first cubist paintings, partly inspired by Cézanne's work.

1926 Monet, the last surviving impressionist, dies in Giverny.

Index